DANCE:
THE MOTION OF
MATH, MUSIC, AND MIND

Matthew He

authorHOUSE®

AuthorHouse™
1663 Liberty Drive
Bloomington, IN 47403
www.authorhouse.com
Phone: 1 (800) 839-8640

Published by AuthorHouse   01/20/2015

ISBN: 978-1-4969-6479-3 (sc)
ISBN: 978-1-4969-6478-6 (e)

Contents

Dance: The Motion Of Math, Music, And Mind

Matthew He

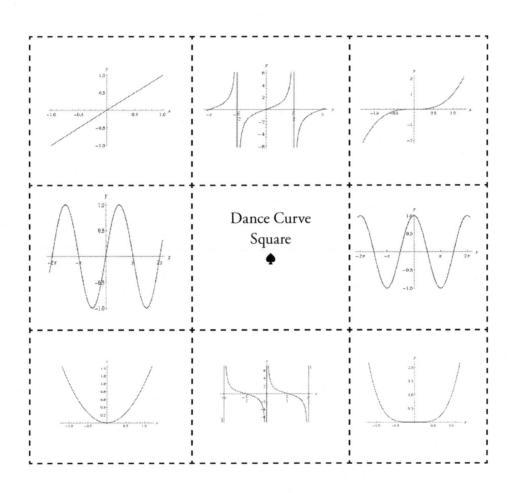

Dance Curve
Square

♠

2015

Dance Equation

$$D\ (t) = \oiiint \{B\ (t) + H\ (t) + M\ (t) + S\ (t)\}\ \partial t$$

Dancing = $\oiiint$	(Body Motion) +	(Heart Emotion) +
	(Mind Expression) +	(Soul Reflection)}∂t

Foreword

Math,
Music,
Mind,
Motion,

On the surface,
Math deals with numbers and symbols;
Music plays with sound and silence;
Dance works with movements and steps.

One may wonder,
Do math, music, and dance communicate?
Are they related to each other?
What are the true intersections among them?

At the first look,
Math is a language of scientific information;
Music shows us patterns and human emotion;
Dance is a language of emotion via physical motion.

Take a closer look,
Dance occupies time and space through pattern organization and creation;
Dance shows artistry in motion reflected by sequence of math shapes and forms;
Dance connects body motion, heart emotion, mind expression, and soul reflection.

Inside this collection,
55 original poems are jotted down on my dance exploration;
What is next?
Move on to book chapters,
Tune in to dance music,
Dance to discover…

Math Dance

Move as music flows and brain waves;
Act not for others but ourselves;
Turn any space into a dance floor;
Hustle around disco without stop.

Music Dance

Music rhythm flows like ocean waves;
Unity of two opposites dances like rainbow curves;
Single dance, partner dance, or group dance…
I dance, you dance, we dance them all;
Circle to the music on the dance floor.

Mind Dance

Mind spins invisibly;
Identity dances naturally;
Neurons move actively;
Dance shows the truth visibly.

Matthew He
Florida
January 15, 2015

Chapter 1

Dance: Variations and Exploration

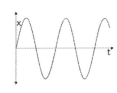

Dance Curves

Differentiable curves move up and down smoothly;
Algebraic curves turn at different direction magically;
Numerical flows simulate the motion approximately;
Cubic curves describe the motion precisely;
Elliptical curves spin around on axis symmetrically.

- ❖ **Elegant Waltz**
- ❖ **Romantic Rumba**
- ❖ **Sexy Salsa**
- ❖ **Fast Quickstep**
- ❖ **Rhythmic Cha-Cha-Cha**
- ❖ **Energetic Swing**
- ❖ **Country Two-Step**
- ❖ **Sporty Disco Hustle**
- ❖ **Passionate Paso Doble**
- ❖ **Sensual Argentina Tango**

Elegant Waltz

One, Two, Three,
Four, Five, Six,
Let's dance a Waltz.

Rise and fall,
Fall and rise,
As light as cloud,
As soft as wind,
As bright as stars,
As ardent as fire,
We flow gently like a sine curve,
We move seamlessly with ups and downs.

Constantly in a circle of wave,
Gracefully around the dance floor,

Waltz, Waltz, Waltz,
One, Two, Three,
Four, Five, Six…

Romantic Rumba

I open my arms gently,
She closes the frame gracefully.

Passionate moves,
Dance of love,

Our footwork are not fancy,
Our body movements are sexy.

Romantic and sensual,
Romantic and lustful.
Our love were once lost,
Rumba got our love found.

We curve our body moves,
As light as soft wind flow,
We breathe to the music,
Our love sparks the magic.
Rumba, Rumba, Rumba,
Slow…, Quick-Quick

Sexy Salsa

Salsa, Salsa, Salsa,
It started from Cuba,
Shall we now Salsa?

Slow, Quick-Quick,
Not only move our hips,
Quick feet are in mix.

Spin, spin, spin,
Turn, turn, turn,
Rhythms are within

Quick turn to the left,
Quick turn to the right,
Salsa on a spot.

Left arm meets right arm,
Right arm holds left arm,
Captivated as dazzling charm.
We dance on the spot,
Salsa to the night,
Salsa never stop.

Quickstep

Quickstep music is playing,
Dancing floor is spinning,
Beautiful couples are flying.
We turn, we hop,
It's rhythmic,
It's energetic,
We are dancing quicksteps,
Brisk pace,
sharp moves,
We are floating on a cloud…

Rhythmic Cha-Cha-Cha

Fast-paced Cha-Cha-Cha,
Originated from hot Cuba.
Cha-Cha-Cha to the left,
Cha-Cha-Cha to the right.
Cha-Cha-Cha back and front,
Cha-Cha-Cha turns round,
It hits my heart beat sound,
I Cha-Cha to the pop,
I Cha-Cha to the rock.
It's authentic,
It's rhythmic,
Cha-Cha to the music.

Energetic Swing

Swing, Swing, Spin, Spin,
Spin, Spin, Swing, Swing.

Swing to the left side,
Spin to the right side.

When a song swings,
We can not stand still.

We can swing to the pop,
We can swing to the rock.

We can swing fast,
We can swing slow.

Swing seamlessly,
Swing freely…

Country Two-Step

I wear my cowboy hat,
She wears cowgirls pants,
We dance country two steps,
Quick-Quick to turn,
Slow-Slow to open,
Move together into a circle,
Travel quickly on the dance floor.
Turn, Turn, Turn,
Round, Round, Round.
Once we start country two-step,
We move and never stop.

Sporty Disco Hustle

Dancing queen is on,
We disco hustle on the floor.

And -one two three,
And-four five six.

I turn around 180°,
She twirls around 360°.

Hustle to open arms,
Hustle to fast spins.
Spin likes a tornado,
Feel likes a whirlpool.

Hustle is not only a disco dance,
Hustle is a sport for exercise.

And -one two three,
And-four five six…

Dancing queen is on,
We disco hustle on the floor.

Passionate Paso Doble

Paso doble, paso doble,
Spanish double double.
I face to her,
She faces to me,

I turns away from her,
She turns away from me

We are full of passion and confrontation,
Occupied by determination and domination.

So many stories to tell,
So much emotion to show.

Paso doble, Paso doble,
We are palpable.

Sensual Argentina Tango

Embrace,
Connect,
Become inseparable.
Balance,
Entangled,
Feel sensual.

We begin to dance,
Rises and falls,
Flows and ebbs,
Lights and shadows, like waves at the shore.
Drawing an ocho eight, like a painter,
Sketching a branch of flowers, like an artist.

Even while the music plays,
Even as dance continues,
Body and soul feel entranced,
The world stops.

Chapter 2

Dance: The Motions of Life

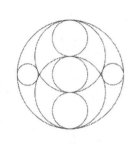

Dance Circle

Diameter of a circle opens a straight dance line widely;
Angle of rotation circle tells dancers to spin around precisely;
Natural circular frequency allows dancer move around frequently;
Circumference of a circle offers dancers a path to move freely;
Equation of a circle traces a dance circle perfectly.

- ❖ **What is Dance?**
- ❖ **Dance: The Motions of Life**
- ❖ **To Dance**
- ❖ **Dance Moves**
- ❖ **Dance: Express with your whole self**
- ❖ **Dance as One**
- ❖ **Dance Dynamics**
- ❖ **Dance: The Motion of Motions**
- ❖ **Dance Movement**
- ❖ **Dance Connects Body, Mind, Heart, and Soul**

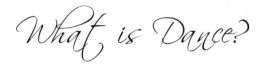

What is Dance?

A dance is a painting of forms,
An orchestra of rhythmic songs.

A dance expresses human movements,
A gateway to the garden of truths.

A dance is like sticks and stones of motion;
A dance is like a shining shell flowing in a blue ocean.

A dance moves to deep insight;
A body moves with its patterns of heart beats.

A dance traces new lines in each familiar face;
A dance shapes its own marvelous place.

Dance: The Motions of Life

Dance: the motions of life,
It connects body, mind, heart, and soul.

Dance: the mathematical patterns in space,
Along with rhythmic music in time.

Dance: a series of comprehensive motions,
It occupies space and time through pattern organization and creation.

Dance: the truest expression of a person,
through body motion, heart emotion, and soul reflection.

To Dance

Explore true nature of body movements;
Experience true rhythm of heart beats;
Empower true power of brain waves;
Examine true spirit of soul patterns;
Embrace true meanings of life pathways…

Dance Moves

A word is made of ordered alphabets.
A dance move begins with basic steps.

When bringing dance to a stop,
it's like a sentence ending with a period.

Dance is the language of movement,
each move is like a word.

The body moves beyond what words can say.
The way people move tells stories the book cannot.

Dance: Express with your whole self

Dance is not just footwork,
It promotes a strong teamwork.

Dances start with basic simplicity,
It varies to complex moves through creativity.

Dance not only pushes physical ability,
It tests one's rhythmic musicality.

Dance can be performed in freestyle,
Yet it requires a great deal of discipline.

Dance can be practiced by yourself,
Yet it presents opportunity for social skills.

While Dance shows artful forms and shapes,
It is supported by physical fitness.

Dance moves and pulses,
It exhibits grace and poise.

Dance is not only a series of comprehensive movements,
It's full of constant enjoyment.

Dance as One

When dancing,
Not only moving your arms or legs;
Not only turning your torso or hips;
Not only raising your head or feet;
All your body parts ought to communicate as a whole;
All your body parts should coordinate with no holes;
All your body parts dance connecting to your heart and soul.

When dancing,
Who is in control of your steps?
What things make your body move?
How does it work?
It's all in your mind;
It's all in your heart;
It's all in your soul…

Dance Dynamics

Dance floor opens up a space gently,
Music play starts with a time smoothly,
Dancers step on the dance floor rhythmically,
Space, time and dancers set the stage dynamically.

Dancers move this way,
Dancers turn that way,
No two dancers dance the same way.
Space and time stayed the same in many ways.
Dance variations interact with relative constants:
Magically they interplay with harmonics.
Space, time, and movements,
Collectively they form a dance dynamics.

Dance: The Motion of Motions

Translation, rotation, reflection,
Are mechanical rigid solid motions.

Tapering, twisting, squeezing,
Are non-rigid elastic motions.

Air flowing, fluid pumping, breathing taking,
Are biochemical fluid motions.

Happiness, sadness, anger,
Are part of psychological emotions.

Solid motion, elastic motion,
Fluid motion, emotional motion,

Dance puts them all into one motion.
Dance: the motion of motions.

Dance Movement

Dance movement,
One of the great laws of life;
The flow of energy inside us,
Like a river all the time.

Dance movement,
Direct mirror of our behavior,
The flow of expression inside us,
Like a book of autobiography we cannot lie.

Dance Connects Body, Mind, Heart, and Soul

Dance is the language of body;
Math is the language of mind;
Music is the language of heart and soul;
All these languages are universal.
Dance is a unique language of all.
Dance transforms space, time, and people;
Dance reflects math patterns as an integral:
Dance interprets music rhythm at a personal level;
Dance communicates the spirit
through body, heart, mind, and soul.

Chapter 3

Dance: The Language of Body

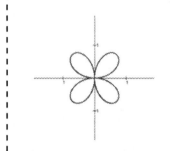

Symmetric Dance

Symmetric **D**igraph flows on its dancing edge symmetrically;
Symmetric **A**lgebra computes its dancing steps precisely;
Symmetric **N**etwork connects its dancing dots symmetrically;
Symmetric **C**enter stays on its dancing position steadily;
Symmetric **E**xpression shows its dancing forms symmetrically.

❖ **Dance is a Language**
❖ **Dance is Like Relationships**
❖ **Dance, Music, and Language**
❖ **Dance in 24 Languages**
❖ **Dance: Cultural Identity**
❖ **Dance is a Verb**
❖ **Dance Types?**
❖ **Dance Alphabet**
❖ **Dance is Like the Number Eight**
❖ **I Dance**

Dance is a Language

Dance begins with basic steps,
Each step is like a letter of the alphabet.

A sequence of steps produces body movement,
Each movement forms a beautiful word.

Each word is pronounced through an internal expression,
Each expression carries interpretative emotion.

Rhythmic movements forms elegant patterns,
Variations of patterns reflect the deep meanings.

Each pattern forms the movement of dictionary,
Dance produces a book of life stories.

Dance is Like Relationships

A dance is like relationships,
It is as much as about your patience,
It is as much as about your kindness,
It is as much as about your confidence.

A dance is like relationships,
One couple may be doing a Waltz,
Another couple may be doing a Foxtrot,
Both are beautiful in their own right.

Dance, Music, and Language

Dance, music, and language;
Socio-ecologically facilitated;
Socio-culturally orchestrated;
Socio-historically instituted.
Dance, music, and languages;
Propagated by socially-embedded brains;
Accumulated through cultural artefacts;
Created by causality between brain, culture, and environments.

Dance in 24 Languages

صقر in Arabic
Танц in Bulgarian
舞蹈 in Chinese
Dans in Dutch
Dance in English
Danse in French
Tanz in German
לוחמ in Hebrew
नृत्य in Hindi
Danza in Italian
ダンス in Japanese
댄스 in Korean
Aliqua in Latin
Бужгийн Mongolian
Dans in Norwegian
Taniec in Polish
Танец in Russian
Danza in Spanish
การเต้นรำ in Thai
Танець in Ukrainian
Khiêu vũ in Vietnamese
Dawns in Welsh
טאנצן in Yiddish
Dance in Zulu

This is only a partial list,
More languages can be added.
Each language looks different,
Yet all represent body movement.

Dance: Cultural Identity

Dance traces back to ancient history.
Dance travels from ballet classical to today's contemporary.

Dance is cultural,
Dance is social.

Dance culture is part of humanity,
Dance movement is part of everyone's identity.

Dance reveals much about the individuality,
Dance conveys much about that community.

Dance is a Verb

Sway, pirouette, gyrate;
Trip, twirl, whirl;

Bop, disco, rock,
Boogie, mosh, groove;

Caper, cavort, frisk,
Frolic, skip, prance,

Gambol, jig; hop
Leap, bounce, jump…
Dance makes the world spin…
Dance makes the world stop.

Dance types?

Solo dance,
Partner dance,
Group dance,

They are not just dance types.
They form individual personality,
partner connectivity, and group community.

Solo dance is a form of individual self-expression,
Partner dance presents pair interaction,
Group dance shows community multi exploration.

Solo dance shows who I am,
Partner dance reflects who we are,
Group dance tells why we are who we are.

Dance Alphabet

A for Allemande
B for Ballet
C for Cha-Cha-Cha
D for Disco
E for Electronic dance
F for Foxtrot
G for Gavote
H for Hip Hop
I for Irish dance
J for Jive
K for Koftos
L for Lambada
M for Merengue
O for One-step
P for Pasodoble
Q for Quickstep
R for Rumba
S for Salsa
T for Tango
U for Ukrainian dance
V for Viennese waltz
W for Waltz
Z for Zydeco
Twenty six letters A to Z;
Each letter except for X and Y
finds a dance genre in its place,
Letters X and Y are vacant
from dance for future play.

Dance Like Number Eight

One, two, three, four,
Five, six, seven, eight.

When you dance out,
Your heart beats number eight.

When you change around your body weight,
Your hips form a curve of eight.

Move front or back, move left or right,
Move all eight directions alright.

Music plays, body moves, heart beats,
Dance moves like number Eight.

I Dance

I dance, smile, and practice,
I perform, create, and express.
I twirl, spin, and leap,
I pirouette, tap, and jump.

I feel, connect, and embrace,
I explore, discover, and experience.
I do not dance because I am happy,
I am happy because I dance.

Chapter 4

Dance: The Artistry in Motion

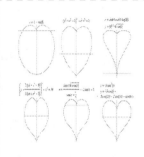

Dance Motion

Deformation of curves flows like a human heart;
Angular motion of equation describes dancing moves;
Normal vibration pumps along with dancing motion;
Circular flow motion continues on dancing with no ending;
E =MC² is hidden behind the dance motion.

- ❖ **Dance: the Artistry in Motion**
- ❖ **Dance: A Multi-medium**
- ❖ **Dance (In a Shape of Pascal Triangle)**
- ❖ **Dancing: Living Painting**
- ❖ **Dance Yin-Yang**
- ❖ **Power of Dance**
- ❖ **Dance Horizontally and Vertically**
- ❖ **Motion Poems**
- ❖ **Dancing: The most living arts**
- ❖ **Dance to the Music**

Dance: the Artistry in Motion

Dancing is the artistry of motion,
It has the additional merit of being human.

Dancing is a painting with hands and eyes;
Dancing is poetry with arms and legs.

The dance can uncover the meanings hidden in music,
It can reveal human emotion through body movement.

Dance: A Multi-medium

Not just to make a physical movement;
Not just to follow the musical rhythm;
Not just to create choreographic postures;
Puts images, sound, and nonverbal texts in motion;
A multi-medium transmitting inner expression.

Dance (In a Shape of Pascal Triangle)

Dance
Just Dance
Dance Connects Us
One Two Three Four
Let Heart Out On the Floor
Move up Get down Sway Around
Young or Old Never Early Never Late
Body Move Heart Beat Five Six Seven Eight

Dancing: Living Painting

Solo, partner, group,
regardless the dance formation;
Classical, modern, ballroom,
regardless the dance genre;
On the dance floor, or performance stage,
regardless where the dance takes place;
Dance is a living painting.

When music starts,
You begin with your movement.
The steps you make,
The breaths you take,
Through every motion you express,
With every curve you draw,
Each live pose is a moment of grace
When the music goes to the last note,
You conclude your move with a final pose.

Dance Yin-Yang

Circle of Yin-Yang,
Unity of two opposites.

Partner dancing,
Lead and follow; follow and lead;
Unity of two opposite intentions.

Left and right;
Right and left;
Unity of opposite directions.

Pull and push;
Push and pull;
Unity of opposite connections.

Love and hate;
Hate and love;
Unity of opposite emotions.

Partner dancing,
Yin-Yang in motion.

Power of Dance

Dance
Power of Dance
Art form for expression
Medium for sensing, learning, and communicating
Possess its own vocabulary, skills, and techniques
Offer creative and critical thinking with kinesthetic abilities

Dance Horizontally and Vertically

DO NOT STOP DANCE
AS IT'S THE MOTIONS OF LIFE
NO MOTION, NO LIFE
CAN NOT STOP DANCEING
EMOTIONAL MOTION IS IN ITS PLACE

Motion Poems

Math describes the dance patterns;
Music produces the dance rhythms;
Mind governs the dance expressions;
Motion composes the dance poems.

Dancing: The most living arts

Music is an art that uses sound and silence,
Sculpture is the art that reflects human intelligence.
Painting is a silent poetry,
Literature is a mirror of society.
Many types of human arts exist,
Dancing is the most living arts of all.

Dance to the Music

Music hits the secret places of the soul,
It travels through body for its feel.

It can be joyful,
It can be chill,

It may make you smile,
It may make you cry,

Whatever you feel,
You put your emotions on the floor.

You may move like an angel;
You may move like Mick Jagger;

Follow your heart,
Reflect your soul,

Dance to the music,
Dance for your life.

Chapter 5

Dance: The Science of Movement

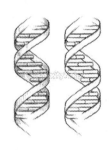

Dance, Dance, and Dance

Directed angle, **D**irected helix, **D**irected circle
Angle of elevation, **A**ngle of deviation, **A**ngle of reflection
Number of combinations, **N**o. of permutations, **N**o. of variations
Concave upward, **C**oncave downward, **C**oncave forward
Euclidean geometry, **E**uclidean Space, **E**uclidean circle

- ❖ **Dance Academics**
- ❖ **Dance Books**
- ❖ **The Elements of Dance: BASTE**
- ❖ **Dance Element: Human Body**
- ❖ **Dance Element: Action**
- ❖ **Dance Element: Space**
- ❖ **Dance Element: Time**
- ❖ **Dance Element: Energy**
- ❖ **Dance as DNA Double Helix**
- ❖ **Waggle Dance**

Dance Academics

Dance: Not just physical movement,
It's full of academics.

Dance has a long history,
Dance travels to all geography.

There is dance notation,
There is dance composition.

Dance is a nonverbal language,
Deeply rooted into its own culture.

Dance is scientifically technical,
Dance is psychologically emotional.

Dance Books

Millions of dance books are there,
Select a few of them here:
Beginning with Understanding dance;
Thinking through the philosophy of dance performance and practices;
Tracing back the history of dance;
Learning complied dance words;
Getting inside of dance anatomy and kinesiology;
Reading the book of dance;
Mastering the dance bible;
Living through dance artistry in motion;
Enjoying elegant ballroom dancing;
Exploring dancing: the pleasure, power and art of movement.

Cited Books:

- *Understanding* Dance, By Graham McFee, 2003
- *Thinking Through Dance: The Philosophy Of Dance Performance And Practices,* By Bunker, Jenny, Anna Pakes and Bonnie Rowell, 2013
- *History of Dance: An Interactive Arts Approach,* By Gayle Kassing, 2007
- *Dance Words,* Valerie Monthland Preston-Dunlop, 1995
- *Dance Anatomy And Kinesiology,* By Karen Sue Clippinger, 2006
- *The Book of Dance,* By Lorrie Mack and Dorling Kindersley, 2012
- *The Dance Bible: The Complete Resource for Aspiring Dancers,* By Camille LeFevre, 2012
- *The Living World of Dance: Artistry in Motion,* By Jack Vartoogian, Linda Vartoogian, Carol Cooper Garey, 1997
- *Ballroom Dancing,* By Alex Moore, 2012
- *Dancing: The Pleasure, Power, and Art of Movement,* By Gerald Jonas, 1992

The Elements of Dance: BASTE

Dance has its own content and skills,
Dance has its own vocabulary and techniques.
What are the dance elements?
They are five letters in a roll: B.A.S.T.E

Body
Action
Space
Time
Energy
The elements of dance are foundational,
Dance sums them up as a whole.

Dance Element: Human Body

Human is born as a moving creature.
In dance, the body is the mobile figure.
The body is felt by the dancer,
Seen by others.
In dance, all our body parts:
Head, eyes, face, shoulders,
fingers, torso, legs, feet,
They coordinate acting as a whole.
In dance, all our body shapes as
symmetrical, rounded, twisted,
angular, linear, nonlinear,
We shift back and forth
between the inner-outer senses of body.
In dance, all our body systems:
muscles, bones, organs,
breath, balance, reflexes,
Connects and integrates.
In dance, all our inner senses,
perceptions, emotions, thoughts,
intentions, imagination, identity,
Reflects and communicates.

Dance Element: Action

Dance is made up of streams
of movement and pauses,
lifts, carries, and catches.
Dance movement originates,
Dance movement creates,
Dance movement evolves.

Dance movement
travels through space:
slide, gallop, hop,
crawl, run, skip,
roll, jump, leap,

Dance movement
also occurs in one spot:
stretch, bend, and rock,
twist, turn, and tip,
rise, fall, and shake.

Dance Element: Space

Dancers interact with space in myriad ways,
Countless variations of ways
that movement can occur in space.
Dancers may stay in one place;
or travel from one place to another place;
Move through personal space or general space.
They may move forward or backward,
right or left, diagonal or sideways,
Their pathways can be curved or
straight, zig-zag or any other ways.
They can be in front or behind,
located under or above,
They can be near or far,
Alone or connected,
Individual and group proximity to object,
in motion or completely still.

Dance Element: Time

Human movement is naturally rhythmic,
Spoken word and conversation
have rhythm and dynamics,
Dance movements may exhibit
different variation and dynamics:
Simultaneous or sequential motion;
Brief or long duration;
Fast or slow speed;
Accents in predictable
or unpredictable intervals.
In dance, the inherent rhythms are in our motion,
Our aural landscape is a rich source of variation.

Dance Element: Energy

Energy: the force of an action;
Both the physical and psychic.
That drives and characterizes motion.
Energy gives force, tension, and weight.
A dancer may step into an arabesque position
with a sharp, percussive attack
or with light, flowing ease.
Energy may change in an instant, and
several types of energy may be concurrently in play.
Energy choices may reveal emotional states.
A powerful push might be aggressive
or playfully boisterous depending on the intent and situation.
A delicate touch might appear affectionate or uncertain,
or perhaps suggest concern.
Some types of energy can be expressed in words,
others spring from the movement itself and are difficult to label with language.
Sometimes differences in the use of energy are easy to perceive;
other times these differences can be quite subtle and ambiguous.
Energy taps into the nonverbal yet deeply communicative realm of dance.

Dance as DNA Double Helix

DNA letter A pairs with letter T,
Letter C pairs with letter G,
They dance around forming a double helix.

They move up and left,
They turn side and right,
They all pair as one unit.

They start together,
They end together,
In between beautifully coiled.

DNA dance can be short,
DAN dance can be long,
Just symmetrically the best.

Waggle Dance

Bee
Bee
Waggle
Waggle bee
Built its own colony
Waggle phase, return phase, Waggle Dance
Running through an elegant figure shape- number eight
…
Dance
Dance
Waggle
Waggle dance
Not only indulgence
It shows distance and direction
Nobel Laureate Frisch once discovered waggle dance
…

Afterword

We Dance Mathematically
We face each other along a **D**iagonal direction;
We turn precisely with 360° **A**ngle of rotation;
We flow continuously like a **N**atural logarithmic function;
We dance together on the floor as a **C**ircle of geometry;
We dance mathematically like of an **E**quation of symmetry.

Two Random Points
We are two random points, once connected;
We form as one flexible segment.
We move like a sine curve, conjugated with a companion cosine wave;
We go up smoothly;
We come down continuously;
We intersect periodically;
We separate congruently;
We dance forward naturally;
We dance backward reversely;
We are not only two random points;
We Waltz 3 steps as one mathematical unit.

We Dance as One Unit
We dance like a unit ball;
We move long on a unit circle.
We dance like a unit cell;
We flow in and out on a unit bi-circle.
We frame as a unit element of a ring;
We dance around a unit of circumference.
We are a unit of normal vector;
We travel on a vector normal field.
We inhale as a unit impulse;
We exhale as a unit of ball.

>>>

Dance to discover,
Dance to explore,
Dance to experience…
When dancing,
Always embrace new adventures,
Take a risk and reveal your hidden talents.

Showing up is more than half of the battle,
Having an open mind is a major part of it,
Pursue it with confidence, and celebrate your curve.

Dance to the music,
Along with the rhythms of your body, heart, mind, and soul,
Enjoy the journey…
Sincere Appreciations to
Dr. Christine Jackson for her constructive comments on poem writing,
Dr. Elana Lanczi for valuable comments on each dance poem,
The entire team at AuthorHouse for prompt guidance and support
throughout the entire process from initial proposal to final publication.
Special thanks to
My dear wife **Axiang** as my dance partner,
Also to my dance teachers, and dance friends…

Matthew He
January 15, 2015
Florida